INSPIRATIONS

By

Jolinda Pizzirani

This is a collection of metaphysical poetry that will touch your heart and stir your soul. These verses speak to the theme of Universal Oneness, spiritual salvation and living your physical life to the fullest while in this realm.

www.SummerlandPublishing.com

First Edition May, 2003

ISBN: 978-0-9794585-1-4

Made in the U.S.A.

Dedicated
to my wonderful family
and dear friends
who light the way
as I travel through this journey.

Also by
Jolinda Pizzirani

"Soul Survivor" is the metaphysical story of a doctor who learns he is dying and decides to participate in an experiment to "prove" life after death. The lives of three different couples are touched —and changed dramatically — by this doctor and his experiences while in an "out of body" state. "Soul Survivor" is a moving, uplifting story which will positively affect every person who reads it.

ISBN 978-0-9794585-0-7 *$15.95*

Available From:

www.SummerlandPublishing.com
www.amazon.com
www.barnesandnoble.com
or your favorite bookstore!

Answers

lie in questions
left unasked
in minds
we least
suspect.

Rise

Rise above life's cruel injustices
Sense your given destiny

Drift away from petty prejudices
Fly with life's old souls

Lift yourself from pain and hatred
Accept a peaceful state

Shun those who are the under miners
Grasp God's gift to you

And you will reach another rung
On life's eternal climb.

To Be

To sometimes sense the feel of love
The texture of it's realness

To learn the breadth of all mankind
And touch our common soulness

To see and be the best we can
Of choices we are given

Is all that we are asked in life
To sense, To Learn, To Be.

Reality

That shady, non-so-sure-of feeling
We rarely grasp or comprehend
That philosophical idealism
Some try to speak of authoritatively
That unpredictable piece of now
That's really past, and future too
That unreal, untold, unknown state
Comprising space universally
That marvelous, wonderful, enticing realm
Ever changing, misunderstood:

Reality!

Our mind's own world
And All That Is.

Love

To love the one you're closest to
The one who shares your life
The one who knows your every whim
Your gladness and your strife

To care about someone so much
You'll happily sacrifice
Things that mean a lot to you
And give them up as vice

To feel the things that they feel
And cry the same wet tears
Sense their true emotions
Grow closer through the years

If you are blessed with these beliefs
and place them far above
Then you are doubly blessed to know
The beautiful meaning of LOVE.

Beginning to End

A newborn's cry
A flower's bloom
A rising sun
New day begun:
These things we praise as new beginnings.

As darkness falls
And flowers fold
A man's last breath
A story untold:
These things we sigh and say our sorrows.

But isn't it reality
To face the fact of humanity?
We all must live
We all must die
And if we believe
In God's true force
Then one's last breath
Starts afterlife's course

So live each day
With goodness of heart
Until The time
you depart

Life's Learning

Slowly, softly, stealthily,
Comes that we might hear nor see;
Trembling, trite, tumultuously,
We face the future with uncertainty;

Unclear, unprovable, out of focus,
The questions mount through eternity;
What could be this strange new state?
Some terrible, horrible, awful fate?

No.
Those with God in their hearts will know:

He waits for us when life is done,
To return to Him as daughter and son;
And show the goals we have fulfilled,
Through years of physical life now stilled;

And if indeed we must return,
It's our decision to relearn
That for which we are to strive,
Before His eyes when in body alive.

Acceptance

For those who pass before us
Their way is always clear
They need not dread nor worry
For there is naught to fear
A year or two or lifetime more
So goes the time we share
Don't waste or wait or contemplate
Just live and show you care.

In Between

When we were small, we had no thoughts
of problems life would bring,

When we grow old, we care no more
of problems life did bring,

It's in between we worry so
of many earthly things,

Why not accept our short time here
with love and understanding,

And clear the way as each day dawns
to Universal Blending.

So Sorry

So sorry we can't accommodate you,
So sorry the truth can't be told

So sorry your reality is so limited,
So sorry life's treasures we hold

For if you learned your real potentials,
Who knows what endeavors you'd try

So better you stay uninformed,
Non believers of whatever's unseen

Stay in your cocoon of safety,
From that which is foreign and mean

But know that one day you'll be ready
To grasp that which lies just ahead

And accept the true word He sends
That Heaven and Earth are One.

Journeys

Through fields of flowers
and remembered sights
In childhood homes and towering heights
Some flying, falling, running times
With myriad colors in our minds
Strangers, family, friends and more
Unknown buildings, misplaced doors
Tears and sadness, happiness too
Clouds and rain, skies of deep blue
Upon awakening all will disappear
Our nighttime journeys become unclear
For our conscious minds can't
comprehend
The lessons which in sleep we tend.

Look, Seek, Believe

Look to the sky for dreams untold
Look to your heart for answers it holds

Seek not your ambition if in greed it lies
Seek your true calling through God's own eyes

Believe in your knowledge of deeds well done
Believe and be sure of your service to His Son.

A Child's Destiny

If we could only but regain
A child's worldly sight again
Before the rest of us destroy
That tenuous tie that is God's joy
But such is not to be the case
We must re-learn the truths we face.

A Basic Truth

To be a basis of some substantiation

To seek a tomorrow of qualification

To know a truth and activation

Is central and basic

to life's justification.

Meditation

Delve deep into your inner self
Search for calm beginnings

Find your special golden thread
A tie to all mankind

Release your conscious mind's abode
Learn your lessons well

For only when we mediate
Deep within ourselves

Is Universal Knowledge shared
With those who love and care.

Of Course

A wish
A guess
A thought
to cope

A life
A sense
Of being
and scope

A now
A then
A future
antidote

And then
Of course
There's Love
and Hope.

Lasting Commitments

A childhood
A life
A Love
A maturity
We share in community

A dream
A cause
A reason
A need
All we believe with impunity

An end
A success
A lesson
And knowledge
All we need for eternity.

Truth

A wave of happiness drifts by untold

Each day we shun our inner souls

For like the clear and flowing tides

So lay our truths 'neath open eyes

Just pray we waken before too long

And rejoice in learning life's true song.

Fleeting Moments

A sudden glance at life's own truth
Leaves one surprised, even bemused,

For peeks and glimpses are shared
at times
To stimulate thoughts and shake
one's mind,

But only if grasped, that tiny thread
Will the meaning of all be heard, unsaid.

A Game Well Played

Alive and well, you seem to be
So why complain — for sympathy?

Enjoy life's triumphs and energies
Savor the lessons and strategies!

It's all a game, well-thought, you see
We've set in motion for you and me.

Misspent Lessons

To come away from all we learn

Like snails with heads that hide, return

To disavow the truth discerned

It's sad but true, we've had our turns

But many shun their lessons learned.

Never Change

I love your thoughts
your words
your being
Your expression of truth
and right
for seeing
So never change
or doubt
or fear
You'll always be strong
in beliefs
others trust.

To Share

Give of what you know the best

Lend that which is needed

Share your knowledge without request

Know that you've succeeded.

Inner Sight

Since the beginning of time there has
been hope
For happiness and health and ways
to cope

But now when we seek that which we
do not know
And answers lie so close to show

We must open our eyes and hearts
and souls
And seek the truth - the words, the goals

And grasp what is right, correct, and just
Don't fear, not hear, just trust your
inner sight

Then believe, and leave the rest to
His Might.

Silver Threads

Slender silver threads of life

Entangle us through happiness and strife

If we dare to make a change

We'll see the undeniable cast of things

But still there's always a way untold

To open doors to the Universal Threshold.

Cynicism

Does it matter?
Does it differ?
Is it real?
Is it now?

Can we feel it, touch it, smell it?
Can we test and document it?

No? Well then, it's simple:
Deny it, file it, ignore and deplore it.

For clearly "everyone" knows it so
That only what's proven can be true.

True Love

To truly love is so ambitious
With complications both real and fictitious;

But those who persevere will find
That efforts made are returned in kind;

So when that soulmate does appear
Give your love without a fear;

For each of you have set in motion
That which leads to true devotion.

Memories

Memories...
We sometimes use
To pass the time and lift the blues

We pick and choose
Which private thoughts
we ought not lose

And maybe even we abuse
So we remember
"altered" views

But still they serve special needs
In helping us learn
from life's past deeds.

Another Day

As I write this, another day is done
And I stop to realize my loss of time:
Time in this reality
To make a difference
To share, to learn
To teach, to understand;
We only have
Such a short time here
Let's strive to accomplish
What we can
Before another day begins.

Enlightenment

Summer, Fall, Winter, Spring
Like the seasons love can bring
Peace, harmony, joy and more
Making many silent hearts sing
Morning, noon, evening, night
Light and darkness bring us sight
Of inner souls we dare not seek
And words we think but dare not speak
Soon the day and time will be
When all will sense the truth we see
And then the final tests begin
For everyone ... and you and me.

Oh, If I Could Only Be Everywhere At Once, All the Time!

I think about the world's activities as I
live out each day,
What other people are doing, seeing,
sensing and feeling — as they may

What a wealth of knowledge and under-
standing must lie beyond my reach
Just because I can't be everywhere at
once, all the time…

A willing student to teach.

Future Paths

A darkened entrance

An unknown cave

Let's light the candle

And see the way

That we must strive

To guide our lives

From hidden corners

Of mind's true self

Yesterday, Today and Tomorrow

Yesterday
It seemed like everything was fine
though often times upsetting
And looking back we're quite aghast at
the ways our plans were heading

Today
Now we've got a firmer grasp
of life's needs and necessities
We know for sure the decisions we make
are leading to prosperity

Tomorrow
Will we be so safe and sure in days
and times to come?
When things will seem much clearer now
that yesterday is done.

Universal Goodness

A wonderful life full of love and hope,
With marriage and children to brighten
our scope;

Then suddenly arise, through
God's own ways,
Insurmountable problems that
fill our days;

Perhaps we must learn through sorrow
and strife,
Lessons and goals we must achieve in
this life;

Though He serves us this turmoil to
try to understand,
In His Universal Goodness must we
take His Hand.

Lifetimes

In this lifetime I am me
a blessed and happy person
body woman, mind afire
with life's potentiality

In this lifetime I am me
Unique and a minority
body man, great aspirations
quite an anomaly

In this lifetime I am me
struggling, lonesome soul
body child, short life in sight
how sad and like reality

In this lifetime I am me
all my lives combined
body wo-man, as have been all
from beginning to eternity

We Are

We live
We love
We learn
We grow

We choose
We develop
We teach
We know

We give
We wait
We smile
We sow

We tend
We nurture
We slow
And then

We go.

Days End

The day is done, my family near,
All fast asleep, and none can hear,
The thoughts I think, the words I write,
Nor contemplate my inner might;

Only in these special moments,
Can I whisper tender truths,
Gathering life's hidden hints
of future paths to be;

So now I lay me down to sleep,
and Pray the Lord my soul to keep,
So I may seek my learning place
Deep in my special inner space.

Deja Vu

Suddenly you know it: you've been this way before,
As seconds tick by slowly, you savor foresight's door,
That lets you glimpse a future that's definitely in your past,
A time you try to nurture, but never seems to last,
Deja vu we call this thing familiar yet so strange
Impossible to understand, yet we know we cannot change.

Life's Harvest

When we first begin to see
the inner truth of reality,

It seems as if we're mired in goo,
too deep to ever believe anew,

But somehow many do succeed
in delving through the layers we seed,

And if it helps us to progress,
then we must strive to learn the rest.

Drifting

A gentle breeze lifts heavy air
Bringing sweet fragrance upon it's wings,
Then clears the mind for visiting places
Far and beyond your normal spaces,

We drift and float through myriad feelings
Hoping and daring to experience
new phases,
And so it goes each day and night
As minds explore our innermost sight.

Life's Mysteries

A moonlit night
A starry sky
Enhance our evening muses;

A sunbeam's warmth
A morning's dew
Push inner thoughts aside;

Yet tender dreams
And midnight schemes
Delude us in our sleep;

So we may fly
And drift carefree
To learn life's mysteries.

Also Available from Summerland Publishing

Jolinda Pizzirani, author of "Soul Survivor," "Inspirations," and "Psychic Princess," now brings us this unique collection of messages directly from the angels for all of us to ponder. Every physical entity can hear angel words, but as a prerequisite they must be open to receiving these messages and of a nature to handle and share them properly. Therefore, Jolinda is merely the transcriptionist in this endeavor, and it is hoped that the material provided within "angel words" will begin to satisfy the hunger you have within you for the many unknown factors abundant in Heaven and on Earth.

"angel words" presents a discussion of subjects suggested by the angels themselves, and in addition answers questions submitted by interested individuals living on Earth today. Future editions of "angel words" will embrace the questions put forth by the readers of this first book, and we will continue until all uncertainties have been calmed. Perhaps, as we travel this journey together, we may begin to more successfully navigate the path that lies ahead. U. S. $14.95 / CAN $19.95 ISBN: 978-0-9794585-3-8

"If Your Day Feels Like a Juggling Act Then It's Time to Slow Down and ***Alphabetize Your Life" by Rona E. Jackson.*** This down-to-earth guide to successful and satisfying living is written from the heart, and imbued with the author's special awareness, compassion, and sense of humor. Her A-Z approach is both unique and thorough. Whether it be relationships, the space you inhabit, self-love, your impact on the planet, or your connection to the universe at large, "Alphabetize Your Life" touches upon it all. Make this book your compass as you journey through life, and you'll always be headed in the right direction.

U. S. $8.95 *ISBN: 978-0-9795444-4-0*

Available Online:
www.SummerlandPublishing.com, www.barnesandnoble.com
or www.amazon.com

www.ingramcontent.com/pod-product-compliance
Lightning Source LLC
LaVergne TN
LVHW020312110826
845148LV00017BA/2640

9780979458514